Violin For Passionate Beginners

Jackson J. Patterson

Introduction

Welcome to the world of the violin, a captivating instrument with a rich history. In this guide, we will explore the intricacies of the violin, from its origins to the art of playing it.

The violin is not just a wooden box with strings; it's a complex masterpiece. As we delve into its anatomy, you'll gain a deep appreciation for the craftsmanship behind this enchanting instrument.

To embark on your violin journey, you'll need more than the instrument itself. Discover the essential accessories that complement the violin, enhancing your playing experience and sound.

When the time comes to choose your own violin, we'll provide you with practical advice to make an informed decision that aligns with your goals and budget.

Maintaining your violin's well-being is crucial. Learn how to care for your instrument, ensuring it stays in optimal condition for years of beautiful music.

To truly make music, you'll need to decipher the language of notes. Explore the fundamentals of musical notation, equipping yourself to interpret and play your favorite pieces.

Mastering the basics of playing is essential. From holding the violin correctly to producing your first notes, this guide will help you establish a strong foundation.

Keeping your violin in tune is vital for creating harmonious melodies. Learn the techniques and tools to ensure your instrument is always pitch-perfect.

Your posture and grip on the violin significantly impact your playing. Discover the proper techniques for holding the instrument, setting yourself up for success.

Throughout your journey, you'll find valuable tips and techniques to enhance your skills and confidence as a budding violinist.

Finally, access the world of sheet music, opening doors to a vast repertoire of songs and compositions for you to explore and play. This guide serves as your compass in the world of the violin, equipping you with the knowledge and skills to begin your musical adventure. So, let's dive into the enchanting world of the violin.

Contents

HISTORY OF THE VIOLIN...1

THE PARTS OF THE VIOLIN 5

VIOLIN ACCESSORIES..9

PRACTICAL ADVICE FOR PURCHASING..............................20

VIOLIN CARE...23

HOW TO READ THE NOTES 32

   Learning the basics...32

HOW TO TUNE THE VIOLIN..67

HOW TO HOLD THE VIOLIN...73

USEFUL TIPS..79

SHEET MUSIC 81

CONCLUSION 102

HISTORY OF THE VIOLIN

The present violin owes its existence to an antiquated instrument known as the lira, used in Europe before the ninth century. It was played in an upstanding position and bowed. The influence of the Arabian rabab and the rebec (which rose in Spain) are additionally found in the violin.

This early stringed instrument advanced after some time in Europe into two separate groups of the instrument: those that were held in the arms and square fit as a fiddle ('lira da braccio') and those that were situated between the legs and molded with slanted shoulders ('lira da gamba'). The two of them delighted in incredible achievement and wide use, however, after some time, the instruments held in the arms turned out to be progressively famous. They prompted the advancement of the violin in and around 1550.

(Figure: LIRA DA GAMBA)

The most popular time of Italian violin making extended from the sixteenth to the eighteenth century. Renowned luthiers incorporated the Guarneri, Amati, da Salo, Ruggieri, and Micheli families alongside

Antonio Stradivari and Jacob Stainer, among others. Although players have safeguarded a significant number of these prized violins as the years progressed, they are restricted and worth enormous sums of money today.

Northern Italy had two districts that exceeded expectations in luthier expertise in the previous piece of this multi-year 'brilliant period' run: Brescia and Cremona. Milan and Venice likewise were significant areas for stringed instrument building. Brescia was the first to develop, and its acclaimed stringed instrument school and workshop reared an age of inventive and profoundly gifted craftsmen.

The credit for the main violin is normally given to a Cremonese luthier named Andrea Amati, who had made his name initially as a lute manufacturer. He made two, three-string violins during the 1540s. He was then dispatched to fabricate one of the initial four-string violins by the rich Medici family during the 1550s. Although the instrument was expected at first for proficient road performers, it turned into the most beloved instrument for distinguished beginners who had cash to spend in the instrument shops.

The two most recent instances of violins that remain today were both made by Amati in the mid-sixteenth century.

Antonio Stradivari, another popular luthier, took in his exchange as a disciple in the workshop of Nicolo Amati, a grandson of Andrea Amati. The latter was dynamic through a great part of the eighteenth century. He included his own disclosures in varnish and body structure to the expertise he picked up in Amati's shop.

The violin turned into a focal piece of the symphony during the 1600s, advanced by authors like Monteverdi.

As the centuries progressed, the violin developed significantly and experienced one significant change. Initially, the neck was shorter, and the instrument had gut strings. A few forms had just three strings. The most major development occurred during the 1800s when an adjustment in the acknowledged contribution of the violin came about with luthier changes to practically all current violins. A centimeter was added to the neck and fingerboard to take into consideration the change, and the bass bar was expanded in weight to take into consideration all the more string strain. Strings are typically made of steel now.

One acclaimed memorable violin is put away today under close watch at the Ashmolean Museum in Oxford, England. Worked by Antonio Stradivari in 1716 and never played, it is protected, because of how his instruments looked and sounded in a like-new condition. This one of a kind and remarkably important violin, called the Messiah-Salabue Stradivarius, left Stradivari's workshop upon the expert's demise in 1737 and went through a few hands before showing up as a gift at the gallery in the twentieth century. As per reports, the blessing accompanied a stipulation that the violin never is played.

Research and experimentation have gone into attempting to reproduce the characteristics of brilliant period violins using current materials and techniques; however, the first instruments are still profoundly valued.

The violin keeps on advancing today with inventive structures in electric violins that can be played with amplification and effects.

Famous Players

The violin isn't just used in old-style music. It is also a well-known sound for jazz, twang, rock, people, and down-home music.

Renowned old-style violin players include Yahudi Menuhin, Pablo de Sarasate, Jascha Heifetz, David Oistrakh, Fritz Kreisler, Giuseppe Tartini, Mischa Elman, Arcangelo Corelli, Joseph Joachim, Itzhak Perlman, Antonio Vivaldi, and even Wolfgang Mozart. Niccolo Paganini is thought by numerous individuals to be a definitive traditional violin player and maker, as he composed and immaculately played out probably the most challenging collection accessible for the violin.

There are numerous eminent jazz violinists, including Stephane Grappelli, Jean Luc-Ponty, Joe Venuti, Ray Nance, Federico Britos, Svend Asmussen, and Regina Carter.

Notable nation and society violinists include Charlie Daniels, Bob Wills, Dale Potter, Spade Cooley, Roy Acuff, Chubby Wise, Tommy Jackson, Vassar Clements, Tommy Vaden, and Alison Krauss.

THE PARTS OF THE VIOLIN

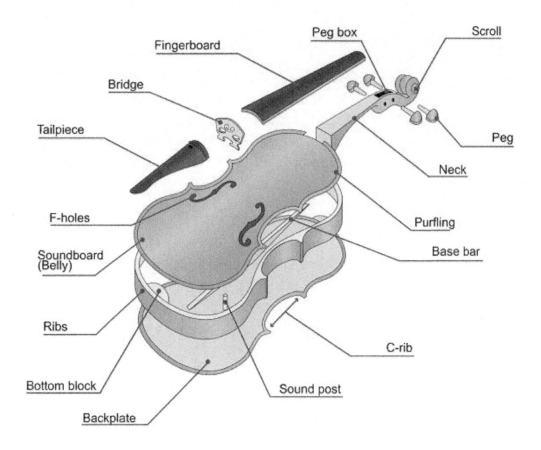

Knowing the names of the various pieces of the violin is basic for any novice, so the player has an idea of what parts they may need to collaborate with to re-tune, restring and take care of their instrument.

Parts of the Violin

1. **Scroll**

The scroll of the violin is the very top of the instrument over the pegbox. Its characteristic curl design resembles a scroll; however, some older instruments have a scroll that is more intricately carved with animals or figures.

2. Tuning Pegs/Pegbox

The tuning pegs and pegbox are situated at the highest point of the instrument by the scroll. This is the place the strings are joined at the top. The end of the string is embedded into an opening in the peg, which is the wound to tighten the string. Most of the tuning is performed by tightening of the peg, with fine tuners being used for strings out by less than half a tone.

3. Nut

This part is the connector between the fingerboard and the peg box. The nut has 4 grooves in it which the strings sit in, so that are appropriately dispersed. If you restring a violin or the strings are loosed, you should make sure the strings are sitting in the grooves at the nut (and at the bridge) before you begin to tighten them.

4. Strings

The part on the violin is tuned G, D, A, E from the lowest to the highest. Strings vary in quality, and the nature of the strings has an impressive effect on the tonal quality delivered by the instrument. Strings are produced using a wide range of metals (primarily aluminum, steel, and gold for the E-string). Nonetheless, some manufactured materials are also used to create strings, and 'catgut' strings made out of animal digestive tracts are still very popular today.

5. Neck

This is the part of the violin that carries the majority of the strings. The neck is the long wooden piece behind the fingerboard, which the fingerboard is stuck to. The neck of the present-day violins is thinner and longer than the neck of the baroque violins.

6. Fingerboard

The fingerboard is the smooth dark playing surface stuck to the neck of the violin underneath the strings. Violinists get dark buildup on their fingers on the left hand because of the black polish rubbing off. Eventually, if this starts to happen, the fingerboard would need refinishing.

7. Body

This part of the violin is the part that intensifies the sound in acoustic violins. This part of the violin can be made of a wide range of woods. While most violins have two-piece backs that are joined together with a seam down the center, one-piece backs are favored because of their increased resonance.

8. Sound Post

This part is the round post inside the violin that runs from the front piece to the back-piece under the scaffold of the violin. The sounding post assumes a key role in how the violin produces sound, and it additionally assists with supporting the structure of the violin from the weight made by the pressure of the strings.

9. F-Holes

After the strings vibration resonates inside the body of the violin, the sound waves are coordinated out of the body through the F-holes. A good tip for beginners is to arrange the F-holes to face your audience. Doing this will allow the audience to hear the perfect sound. Obviously, you don't have to stress over this if you play an electric violin, or if you are playing with a pick-up.

10. Bridge

The bridge of the violin comes in fluctuating angles of the bend. A smaller edge makes it simpler to play twofold or triple stops (playing two or three strings simultaneously.) Whereas progressively bent extensions make it simpler to hit the correct notes without scraping over an off-base string. Old style violinists will, in general, have increasingly bent bridges. Country players or fiddles have flatter bridges. This bridge also has ridges on it that help to space the strings out evenly. On great quality E-strings, a little plastic cylinder should be folded over the string. This should be placed over the extension to prevent the small E-string from cutting into the wood.

11. Fine Tuners

Fine tuners can be found either on each of the four strings, or simply the E string. If you are a beginner, you should pick a violin with four fine tuners as it makes it less common that you will break a string while tuning. Fine tuners are a screw that presses down a switch that fixes the string partially. Where a fine tuner arrives at the end of the screw, it should be unscrewed totally, and the peg should be tightened before using the fine tuner again.

12. Tailpiece/Endpin.

The tailpiece is what the strings are joined to at the base of the instrument, nearest to the player's chin. The tailpiece is joined to the base of the instrument by the endpin or end button, a little button on the violin that rubs against the player's neck.

VIOLIN ACCESSORIES

1. The Bow

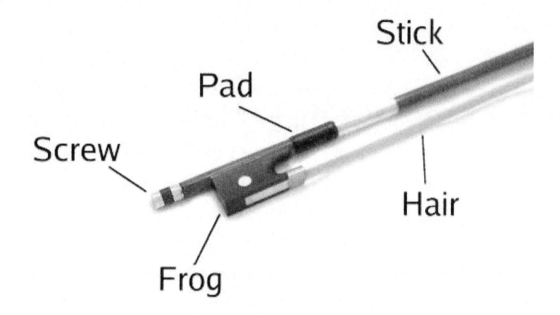

T he bow is one of the important violin accessories. It is used to create the sounds we appreciate hearing by moving it over the strings. The bow is comprised of five sections that work together; it holds the hair, which is moved over the violin's strings.

There are various sorts of bows for violins, but they basically work a similar way. The hair connected to violin bows is typically taken from horses. To get the best impact while using the bow, it is important that the hair is appropriately fixed and held in position with the screw. Fixing the bow hair too close may cause a few issues while playing the violin.

Another factor that influences the sounds created when using the bow is the pressure you put on the strings during training. After some time, adhering to a specialist violinist's directions, you should become familiar with the pressure that needs to be used when bowing.

Parts Of The Bow

Screw.

This part of the bow is on the end of the frog, which fixes and loosens the hair. If the screw on the end of the frog is unscrewed, the frog falls off the bow (it is not difficult to reattach) when the screw is fixed it extends the hair of the bow nearer to the end of the bow, tightening the strain of the hairs.

Hair

This part of the bow is the part that contacts the string when playing. Normally the hair is made out of either a manufactured material or horsehair, and these strands should be rosined to create sound. If your bow isn't rosined, you may find that it slips on the string and creates a gentler, whisper-like tone

Frog

The frog is the piece of the bow that the violinist holds. The frog is the place all the mechanics of the bow occur.

Pad

The pad of the bow helps the player to hold the bow.

Stick

The main stick of the bow is typically made of wood, sometimes with a metal core. The stick should be supple and bendy to have the option to help the tightening and disengaging of the bow hair. A good bow should be light and have a balance point (where you can adjust the bow on one finger) around a quarter of the way up the bow from the frog. The balance point is significant as it permits the violinist to perform propelled specialized developments like spiccato (which is where the bow bounces off the string between each note).

2. Case and gig bag

The case and gig bags are those great carriers used to store the violin and its accessories. Cases for violins come in various structures. You can find cases for violins with various highlights to make it simpler to store your preferred musical instrument.

Depending upon what you need, you can choose to pick a case and gig bag based upon its features. For people who travel often to perform gigs, it is important to use case and gig sacks to accommodate the violin and all its basic accessories. For instance, you can find cases and gig bags with compartments to store more than one violin bow.

These cases for violins also make it really easy to carry the violin. You also need them to shield your violin from bad weather, as they are usually waterproof.

3. Chinrest

The chin rest provides a comfortable pad for putting your chin on while playing the violin. It is connected to the violin. The chin rest is one of the violin accessories that was created after the violin became one of the most widely used instruments in entertainment.

The need to create a chin rest for the violin became fundamental when it was found that playing violins for extended periods can be a serious weight and cause strain on the chin. To stop the chin becoming sore, chin rests were acknowledged by the music network and executed in the violin's design.

The chin rest is also useful when you have to play a vivacious passage in music. This is typically the situation when violins are played in orchestras or during the making of instrumentals for motion pictures. There are various kinds of chin rests for violins, but they all fit completely over the instrument's tailpiece.

4. Maintenance kits

The support packs for violins are lightweight bearer bags that hold the fundamental items used to keep the violin clean and in an ideal functional condition. The normal items found in a violin upkeep pack include natural cleaners (which are okay for the environment), cleaning fabrics, cleaning items, and rosins, which are used to keep the bow hairs in good working condition.

Dust or moisture, can ruin the violin. The things found in maintenance kits can be used to keep this from happening. For instance, the outside of the violin can be shielded from the destructive impacts of dampness by finishing with a decent waxing item for wood surfaces. Using the items found in this pack is simple; the producers also include instruction books to guide you.

5. Pickups and preamps

The pickup and preamps are violin accessories used to deal with wear and tear signs during practices or live concerts. With the assistance of these extras, you can guarantee the correct pitch is enhanced to support your sound.

While playing the violin, you may see the creation of sounds that have low notes. These sounds created from the pickups can adjust your exhibition. The aim is to use a preamp to support the low motions toward a satisfactory level.

Pickups and preamps can likewise be used to improve the nature of notes from the enhancers. Some settings can be used to accomplish this capacity. The volume controls can be used to get the best quality notes when playing the violin.

Pickup and preamps are associated with the intensifiers. Their functionalities include the volume control, equalizer capacities for bass, treble, and mid sounds, adjusting the stages while playing the violin and taking out problematic clamor during violin practice.

Pickups and preamps are also used to blend various notes sent through the speaker. These notes are consolidated to make one note. This capacity will be handy if the preamp you have can deal with numerous channels.

6. Violin Rosin

Rosins are used to keep up the bow hairs of the violin. They are resin materials which have exceptionally frictional surfaces. The rosins come in various brands.

During a presentation with the violin, it is normal to discover that the bow hairs move off the violin strings. The outcome is a twisted sound; experienced violinists can defeat this issue without having an awful execution.

The rosins are used to keep such a circumstance from occurring. They are scoured on the bow hair to improve rubbing. After using rosins on the violin bow hair, you will see that it is simpler to accomplish a firmer grasp on the strings while playing the violin.

Rosins help violinists to accomplish the degree of vibration required while playing the violin. Rosins are easy to use, and it is important for brand new violins bows to be prepped with rosin before the first use.

7. Shoulder Rests

The shoulder rests are basic violin accessories that were created due to genuine need. The older composers discovered it was extremely unpleasant to play the violin for extended periods because of the strain on their shoulders.

Shoulder rests give a cushion that make you feel more comfortable while playing the violin. These accessories are produced using plastic materials, fiber, or wood. They have contours that mold to your shoulders.

You may need to try various kinds to decide which is best for you. Rests are made for violins with screws and are made with flexible features so that they can work for adults or children with no issue.

8. Violin string

New violins come with strings from the producer. However, you may need to have additional violin strings that can be put away in your gig bag until required. The violin strings can last for a long time and have various features depending on your style of music, so you made need to have different strings to accommodate this.

The various features of violin strings show why they produce a differing pitch when played with a bow. Some straightforward features of the string are down to the material it has been made with, its pressure center material, measure and limit, and the material that has been used to cover the string.

Some violin strings sold by respectable brands have been marked. This makes it simple for you to find the data to find out the kind of pitch that you should expect when using the string. Your decision of string will be dependant on the kind of pitch you have to make.

9. Tailpiece

This is the part of a violin that makes sure one end of the string doesn't move.The tailpiece also impacts the nature of pitch created by the violin when it is played. The situation of a tailpiece can also be changed following the right errors in the sounds and vibration.

You can use the rear end to play the correct notes to accomplish an ideal amicability for your tune. The rear end can also be used to improve reverberation, which positively affects the sounds. It is normal to discover violinists with more than one rear end for their situation and gig sacks. This happens when they find specific tailpieces that are generally reasonable for symphony, solo exhibitions, or when playing music.

The tailpiece is produced using wood; they are additionally intended to make the violin look wonderful. The weight of a tailpiece is also a factor that impacts the sound. Lighter rear ends can obstruct you from getting the correct degree of vibrations when playing the violin. You can also adjust the tones created when playing your violin by picking a tailpiece with an appropriate length.

10. Tuning peg and fitting

These are violin accessories used to hold the strings and make the correct pressure before playing the instrument. Tuning pegs are adjustable; however, their use techniques can be precarious when handled by amateurs.

The tuning pegs are used to make the strings tighter or slackened when essential. The pegs have tightened holes that hold the strings firm. Tuning the violin is finished by turning the tuning pegs or moving them appropriately.

The fitting procedure assists with guaranteeing the strings are appropriately extended. During this procedure, keeping up the correct pressure is imperative to abstain from contorting the tones created while playing your violin.

There are A, D, E, and G strings on the violin. These are the strings that are changed by getting the correct pressure using the tuning pegs. To maintain a strategic distance from issues when using tuning pegs, it is essential to keep the pegs greased up before use. While tuning the strings, you can keep up a consistent offset with the tuning pegs by using a decent peg paste.

11. Violin Bridge

The violin bridge is the piece of the instrument that holds the strings. It serves numerous capacities, which help you get the correct tones while playing the violin. The violin bridge is made of wood, and it has various shapes.

The upper part of the bridge is angled. One piece of this curve is higher than the other; they are used to hold the G and E strings. You should set the G string in the higher side of the extension, and the E string goes into the lower angled part.

The extension assists with transmitting the vibrations made by the bow hairs through the soundboard, and this is the thing that we hear as violin sounds. The weight of the strings on the extension holds it set up while the instrument is being used. To prevent lost vibration, it is important to use a violin bridge to keep the string from going into the wood.

12. Violin Mute

The mute is one of the basic violin accessories everybody needs. It is utilized to bring down the pitch delivered by the violin when it is played in an open spot. The mute brings down the violin's pitch to stop you from disturbing others around you. However, you can still hear the pitch to guarantee you are getting the correct notes while practicing.

There are various sorts of mutes; they are fundamentally separated by the materials that they're made of. You should add your mute to the extension of your violin. Apprentices are encouraged to begin with elastic quiets to prevent harming the extension.

To fix the mute on the violin bridge, there is no compelling reason to remove the strings. You can put it over the scaffold with the elastic tubing facing upwards. Make sure the score is made sure over the scaffold to keep your mute from tumbling off while you practice with the violin.

13. Tuner

This is one of the common accessories that is frequently used before training meetings. It is used to tune the strings of the violin to get the correct notes. The violin tuner changes the violin strings, G, D, An, and E, to coordinate the tunes or melodic execution you need to make.

The turners are generally used after the tuning pegs have been used to change the strings. Its capacity is to adjust the strings, however, to prevent breaking the strings, it is essential to make minor changes while using the tuner. If the correct tune isn't accomplished, you can roll out another minor improvement until you get the right results.

You can also use the instructions when using the tuner to get the best pitch.

14. Stand and hanger

The stand and hanger for violins are used to hold the instrument up when you take a break during practicing. The stands are used to help the violin while you can put your bow on the holder.

There are various kinds of stands and holders. If you are rehearsing in a group, you can pick models that can hold at least two violins. Some of these accessories also have holders for sheet music.

Stands and holders are built to have a strong base; this makes the odds of returning to discover your violin on the ground extremely thin. For apprentices, using a holder for sheet music helps during practices. You can put your sheet music on the holder to give you good visibility whilst also holding your violin. The sheet music holder should also be movable, so that it can be used by adults and children alike.

15. Fingerboard and Tapes

This is a common accessory found with instruments, such as the violin that is played using bows. It is produced using wood; fingerboards support the violin strings, which run over it from one end of the instrument to the next.

To get the best outcomes, fingerboards should have a smooth surface without breaks or imprints. It should be easy to slide your fingers from one end of the board to the next while playing your violin. On the fingerboard, there is a sunken impression. This arrangement makes it feasible for the vibrations to happen while playing with a bow.

Fingerboards come in different lengths; you will find shorter forms on violins made for smaller children.

16. Violin humidifiers

These basic accessories keep the humidity around your violin and the bows stable when they are stored. The humidifiers are set for your case and gig bags or a room where you store your violin. You should use the violin humidifiers during travel or a long stockpiling. With the violin humidifiers, half of your activity is done; you won't have to monitor humid conditions to keep your violin fit as a fiddle.

If you live in zones with a dry climate, it is critical to use the violin humidifiers at regular intervals. The standard moist condition for a violin is halved when using a hygrometer for estimation; if you can keep up this condition, your violin won't break. Sticky conditions can be unusual, so using a violin humidifier is significant.

Choosing the Best Violin Parts

In business sectors, there are huge numbers of brands of violin accessories. It might be overwhelming when you need to pick among these brands. If they have been around for some time, you can find reviews from past clients on the web. The distinctive violin accessories that you will be encouraged to purchase have been intended to improve your experience while playing the instrument.

Fortunately, a portion of these violin accessories are produced using strong materials. For instance, you can use the shoulder rests, gig sacks, and withdraws for years after purchase. Depending upon your requirements, you may need to purchase different accessories. This is normally the situation where the accessories for your violin have various features that make the instrument produce differing sounds. For instance, the violin strings can create various pitches relying upon their center and materials.

The primary violin accessories are easy to use; it improves when you are figuring out how to play the violin from an online course. You can take exercises that give information about these accessories.

PRACTICAL ADVICE FOR PURCHASING

1. PURCHASE FROM A REPUTABLE, APPROVED MUSIC STORE, INSTRUMENT DEALER OR LUTHIER

Despite the fact that you can discover incredible, online deals, the web isn't the best place to buy a violin except if you're purchasing another instrument, from a creditable online source - with a reasonable merchandise exchange. For instance, here at Connolly Music, we sell great Revelle violins, all with a two-year guarantee. Experienced artists realize it's important to play your violin with a trained luthier or music store proficient available to respond to any inquiries or worries that emerge before settling on a last decision. If you feel you've gone over an incredible second-hand violin available to be purchased, play it safe. Contact a neighborhood luthier and check whether you can pay him/her a flat fee in return for meeting you at the dealer's to confirm the instrument's condition and relative worth. Or have the merchant meet you at a music store you trust and pay the store to play out a structural investigation and value confirmation.

With the second-hand alternative, you do without two significant advantages of buying a violin from an authentic seller: a guarantee and a money-back promise in case you're not fulfilled. Most music stores sell great quality, second-hand instruments at a competitive cost, and they give these significant post-deal benefits.

2. PLAY THE VIOLIN (AND BOWS) AHEAD OF TIME

Every violin has its own, different sound and character. Even violins made by a portion of the world's most prominent violin producers ever (Stradivari, Amati and Guarneri) sound different to each other. Also, an instrument that sounds and feels good to you may not sound and feel good to the individual selling it or another purchaser. Picking a violin is an individual decision, so it's important that you have plentiful opportunity to explore different avenues regarding it early, to get an exact feel for it. Try not to listen to any other individual's assessment but your own during this procedure. It's your decision, and you'll take advantage of your new violin if you feel a bond or association with the manner in which it feels and sounds to your body and ears.

3. CONFIRM THE RETURN POLICY

Ideally, you'd evaluate a few violins, choose the one that best suits your size, capacity, and inclination, and that would be that. On occasion, however, that is not the case. With online violin purchases, you need some time with the planned instrument(s) to locate 'the one'.

Consequently, most notable violin venders offer some rendition of an arrival policy. Policy terms may differ, however preferably you should have the option to restore the violin (in a similar condition as it was the point at which you bought it) anytime between the range of 14-and 30-days from the original buy date, for a full refund.

4. THE VIOLIN SHOULD ALWAYS HAVE SOME TYPE OF WARRANTY IN PLACE

A brand new violin should accompany a guarantee of some sort. 1-year would be a minimum and the perfect would be a 2-year guarantee or more. These guarantees don't cover harm caused after the purchase (that is the place instrument protection comes in and we'll address that next).

A violin guarantee covers any workmanship and materials that rise after some time. These guarantees regularly stretch out to the first proprietor and don't move to new proprietor should you buy the instrument second-hand. Once more, recycled instruments might not have guarantees accessible except if they're sold by a seller who offers a limited version base on their affirmation of the instrument's condition.

5. BUY INSTRUMENT INSURANCE ASAP

If your instrument and equipment cost $1000 or more, instrument protection is an astute decision. You'll pay just 10% or so of your instrument's worth every year, which is a little cost to pay if you think about the potential cost of loss or theft. At the point when you recognize what to search for in a violin, and you apply these tips all through the choice procedure, you can confidently look for your instrument. When you bring the new violin home, you'll breathe a sigh of relief realizing the exchange is supported with return guarantee, and protection intended to secure you if something goes wrong. Now it's an ideal opportunity to get shopping.

VIOLIN CARE

We realize that violins can survive a hundred years and we are not simply discussing Stradivari or Guarneri or Amati instruments. It applies to any violin (including yours) if you take great care of it.

We are not generally shown basic data on our violins, particularly about appropriate violin care.

We overlook that it should be kept up, and in some cases, the vast majority of us get excessively apathetic to simply clearing the residue off the violin.

1. Invest In A Good Quality Violin Case

The initial step in caring for a violin is to get a decent violin case. It should be tough and made with higher-performing materials.

You should also be able to tie your violin by the neck to keep it secure whilst travelling.

It is essential to keep the case filled with a lot of padding to prevent getting scratches on the violin.

Paddings should cushion the violin, but not to the point where it rubs against the varnish with force.

2. Wipe And Clean Rosin Off The Strings And The Violin After Every Use

The white dust on the violin after playing is called rosin dust. Any rosin left over the body or on the strings of your violin can stick to the instrument and cause it to be clingy/messy.

This will demolish the completion of your instrument, and you will eventually need to get it re-varnished if you don't clean it appropriately.

How to clean the violin body and strings?

Use a lint-free, delicate fabric to clear off the rosin residue to clean your violin. Numerous violin stores sell modest fabric or violin care packs that are perfect for cleaning your violin.

3. Do Not Put Too Much Rosin On The Bow Hair

An excess of rosin on a bow may bring about a harsher and scratchier sound since an excess of contact is made between the bow and the violin string.

Although the excess rosin can fall off while playing, it may adhere to the violin's body and result in a sticky feel on its surface. This means there will be more cleaning to do.

An abundance of rosin may also shorten the life expectancy of the bow hair. Re-hairing is costly, and we don't need extra costs.

4. Do Not Use Alcohol Or Solvents In Cleaning Your Violin

Never use liquor or any cleaning solvents to clean your instrument; they can strip your violin's varnish. Even hot water can hurt your violin.

If you are strictly cleaning or dealing with the violin, you don't have to use anything other than a delicate dry fabric. Some violinists advise the usage of wood polish made for the violin. This is okay if you have the extra money in your pocket, however, in so doing, make sure you use a separate cloth than your usual cleaning cloth to polish your instrument.

5. Keep The Bow Rosin Free After Playing

Following short periods of violin playing, you may be pondering how to clean a violin bow.

As a rule, violin bows are treated with a similar varnish as the violin (particularly when purchased together).

This means you can use a similar dry, delicate material in cleaning the violin to clear the rosin off the wood part of the bow.

6. Keep The Violin In Case When Not In Use

Continuously put your violin inside the case when you are not playing. Never leave it on a seat or table or hanging somewhere like your music stand.

When your violin isn't in its case, it may be accidentally knocked over, sat on, or stood on.

7. Put The Violin In A Place With Appropriate Temperature Levels

Do you live somewhere with very cold temperatures or with a really dry atmosphere?

If yes, ensure your violin case has features to manage these outrageous temperature levels and never leave your violin outside!

8. Make Sure You Use A Humidifier If You Are Storing Your Violin In Cold Places

Your violin set is made out of natural materials. If the wood dries out a lot during low-temperature levels, it may be weaker and have splits in the wood.

Humidifiers like the 'Dampit' can prevent broad drying. More often than not, top-notch violin cases have built in humidifiers.

9. Store The Violin In A Safe Place, Away From Harm

It probably won't be sufficient just to place your violin in its case all the time, so make sure you always store it appropriately.

Try not to store your case somewhere undependable because your violin can get wet or be spilled.

How to store a violin?

The case should be face-up, or on its side. Never put your violin lying on its bridge, even when inside the case, the weight coupled with the high pressure of the strings can make the wood debilitate.

10. Keep Your Pegs Fitted At All Times

Each violin is intended to be played with a lot of well-fitted tuning pegs. Otherwise, you won't have the option to tune the instrument accurately.

If your pegs stick or are difficult to tune, apply a piece of a 'peg dope' onto the region of the tuning peg that is in contact with the violin opening.

This will make the pegs to move more uninhibitedly.

On the other hand, if your pegs slip when you attempt to tune your violin, it's the ideal opportunity for a violin specialist's examination!

You may take your violin to a luthier, and he/she will have your pegs suitably fitted.

11. Always Check Your Bridge's Alignment

The bridge will lean forward if the strings are excessively close. To fix it, cautiously adjust the bridge and ensure that the bridge's feet are level against the outside of the violin.

Keep in mind, if the violin bridge falls, the sound post inside the violin may fall also.

Additional tip: Don't neglect to release your strings marginally before you move your bridge.

12. Clean And Wind The Strings Properly

How to clean violin strings and keep them fittingly twisted?

You have to relax your violin strings marginally. At that point, with a delicate fabric, you can wipe the abundant dust from the string.

Also, make certain to wind the strings effectively. Inconsistencies in the establishment/winding, can split the pegbox and should be avoided.

13. Use Appropriate Violin Fittings

Violin fittings include tuning pegs, chinrest, and tailpiece. Using appropriate pegs for your violin helps guarantee that you will invest less energy managing peg slippage.

With regards to chinrests, if your jawline rest is contacting your violin's rear end, it will cause an irritating humming clamor. If it is excessively large, it may scratch the violin on the opposite side.

If you have four fine tuners on a wooden tailpiece, this will be substantial.

The unfriendly impact of this is it mutes the tone of your violin and exchanges its sound. This is the motivation behind why groups of violin players simply have a couple of fine tuners.

Picking the right tailpiece has a major effect on the sound of your violin.

If you need to use four fine tuners for simple tuning yet additionally need to keep the first stable of your violin, consider using a plastic end with coordinated fine tuners rather than a wooden one.

14. Make Sure You Loosen The Bow When Not In Use

Always disengage the tension of the bow hair after each practice session.

Why? Since the violin bow can lose a portion of its camber if you don't.

It means that if you don't disengage your bow routinely after to playing, the pressure makes the stick twist after some time, losing its raised or curved shape.

15. Keep Your Hands Clean (And Nails Properly-Trimmed)

Have you seen that the hair of your bow is grimy close to the frog? This is the dirt from your fingers.

To keep the bow hair clean, abstain from contacting the hair with your hands. The natural oils that your skin secretes neutralize the holding impact of the rosin.

16. Support The Neck When Adjusting The Pegs

When you are changing your violin's tune with your pegs, you consistently bolster the neck and some portion of your violin with your other hand.

This is done to diminish the danger of snapping your violin's neck.

17. Get Your Bow Re-haired

Re-hairing relies upon the amount you play your violin, the vast majority who play 2-4 hours per day get their bow re-haired consistently.

If you are losing a ton of bow hair, consider getting your violin bow re-haired, so you can prevent the bow twisting.

18. Change Your Violin Strings As Needed

Changing violin strings time after time can be very costly and may not be fundamental. But not supplanting them when they should be can bring about a few disadvantages and can be intense.

Specialists practice changing violin strings at whatever point they look frayed, as there is a higher possibility that they may break while practicing or during a presentation.

To change strings, do it each, in turn, to keep up the strain over the extension.

If you remove all the strings simultaneously, the extension and the sound post may fall over.

19. Do Not Touch The Varnished Parts With Sweaty Hands

Your fingers have oils originating from the organs that can respond and take the varnish off of your violin.

Knowing this, you should avoid contacting the violin with sweat-soaked hands or just hold it by the neck and chinrest.

20. Do Not Use Glue To Mend Any Parts Of Your Violin

Never use a stick that you can buy anywhere for your violin. Violins are created using an exceptional, frail shroud stick.

This paste permits the violin to inhale appropriately during various climate conditions.

Go to a luthier if you feel that your violin has parts that need sticking or fixing.

21. Always Check The Sound Post

Check whether the sound post of your violin is in the right position or if it has tumbled down.

If it has tumbled down, take your violin to a luthier, and they will reset the post and spot it in the right position.

22. Visit A Luthier

Just as you bring yourself or anybody from your family to the specialist for a check up, your violin should be brought to a violin producer or luthier to keep it fit as a fiddle and for it to be cleaned and kept up.

They are the ones who know how to deal with a violin appropriately. You can ask them inquiries, and you can get some information about ways to deal with a violin.

There are numerous violin making/fixing apparatuses that you can't find with anyone else.

When in doubt, if you are not sure of something with your violin, ask a violin master like luthiers to avoid committing errors and to prevent harming your violin and bow.

Never overlook minor issues in the violin since it can turn into a significant issue if left.

Keeping your violin in great condition can help keep up its tone, security, and its worth.

As a violinist, your duty isn't limited to working on, doing practices, and acting before the group, but also in cleaning and taking great care of the violin.

HOW TO READ THE NOTES

Learning the basics

1. Get a handle on the staff.

Before you are prepared to begin learning music, you should get a sense of the fundamental data that essentially every individual who peruses music has to know. The even lines on a bit of music make up the staff. This is the most fundamental of every melodic image and the establishment for everything that is to follow.

- The staff is an arrangement of five equal lines and the spaces between them. The two lines and spaces are numbered for reference purposes and are constantly tallied from most reduced (base of the staff) to most noteworthy (top of the staff).

2. Start with the treble clef.

One of the primary things you'll experience when perusing music is the clef. This note, which resembles a major, extravagant cursive image at the left-hand side of the staff, is the legend that lets you know roughly what run your instrument will play in. All instruments and voices in the higher reaches use the treble clef, and for this introduction to understanding music, we'll center fundamentally around this clef for our models.

- The treble clef, or G clef, is from a fancy Latin letter G. One great approach to remember this is the line at the focal point of the clef's 'twirl' folds over the line that speaks to the note G. If notes are added to the staff in the treble clef, they should have the following qualities:

- The five lines, from the base up, speak to the accompanying notes: E G B D F.

- The four spaces, from the base up, speak to these notes: F A C E.

- This may appear to be a great deal to remember, however, you can use mental aides to assist you with remembering them. For the lines, 'Each Good Boy Does Fine' is a well-known mental helper, and the spaces explain the

'Boy Does Fine' is a common mnemonic, and the spaces spell out the word 'name'. Another great way to reinforce these connections is to practice using an online note recognition device.

3. Understand the bass clef. The bass clef, otherwise called the F clef, is used for instruments in the lower registers, including the left hand of the piano, low pitch guitar, trombone, etc.

- The name 'F clef' gets its roots from the gothic letter F. The two dabs on the clef lie above and beneath the 'F' line on the staff. The staff of the bass clef speaks to unexpected notes in comparison to that of the treble clef.

- The five lines, base to top, speak to these notes: G B D F A ('Good Boys Don't Fool Around').

- The four spaces, base to top, speak to these notes: A C E G ('All Cows Eat Grass').

4. Learn the parts of a note.

Singular note images are a mix of up to three essential components: the note head, the stem, and banners.

- The note head is an oval shape that is either open (white) or shut (dark). At its generally essential, it tells the musician what note to play on their instrument.

- The Stem is the thin vertical line appended to the head of the note. When the stem points up, it joins to the head of the note on the right side. When the stem points down, the head of the note is joined to the left. The stem's direction doesn't affect the note. However, it makes notation less cluttered and easier to read.

- The rule on stem direction is that at the centerline or above it (D for bass clef or B for treble clef) of the staff, the stem points down, and when the note is underneath the middle of the staff, the stem points up.

- The flag is the curved stroke fixed at the end of the stem. Whether the stem is attached to the right or left of the head of the note, the flag is always drawn to the right and never to the left!

- Taken together, the stem, flag, or flags, and the note show the musician the time value for any given note, as expressed in beats or fractions of beats. When you listen to music, and you're tapping your foot in time to the music, you recognize that beat.

Reading Meter and Time

Learn about measure lines. On a sheet music, you will see thin vertical lines crossing the staff at fairly regular intervals. These lines signify measures called 'bars'; the first measure is the space before the first line, the space between the first and second lines, is the second measure. Measure lines do not affect how the music sounds, but they help the performer keep their place in the music.

Another useful thing about steps, as we shall see below, is that each one gets the same number of beats. For instance, if you find yourself tapping

'1-2-3-4' along with a piece of music on the radio, you have probably already found the measure lines subconsciously.

Learn about timing or meter.

Meter can be thought of as the 'beat' of the music. You feel it naturally when you tune in to music; the 'blast, tiss, blast, tiss' of a cliché dance track is a straightforward case of the meter.

- On a bit of sheet music, the beat is communicated by something that appears as though a portion composed close to the main clef image. Like any division, there is a numerator and a denominator. The numerator, written in the best two spaces of the staff, reveals the number of beats in one measure. The denominator discloses the note esteem that gets one beat (the 'beat' that you tap your toe to).

- Perhaps the least demanding meter to comprehend is 4/4 time or 'normal' time. There are 4 beats in each measure, and each quarter note is equivalent to one beat. This is the timing scheme you'll hear in most well-known music. You can tally along to regular time music by checking 'ONE two three four, ONE two three four...' to the beat.

- Changing the numerator, we can change the number of beats in a measure. Another exceptionally regular timing scheme is 3/4. For instance, most dances will have a consistent 'ONE two three, ONE two three' beat, making them 3/4.

- Some meters will appear with a letter C rather than two numbers. 4/4 time regularly appears as a major C, which represents normal time. In like manner, 2/2 meter is regularly shown as a major C with a vertical line through it. The C with the line through it represents cut time (some of the time alluded to as half regular time).

Learning Rhythm

Get in the groove. Since it joins meter and time, 'beat' is a pivotal piece of how the music feels. Be that as it may, while meter reveals to you what number of beats, musicality is how those beats are used.

- Try this: tap your finger around your work area, and tally 1-2-3-4, 1-2-3-4, consistently. Not interesting, right? Now attempt this: tap gentler on beats 1 and 3, tap stronger on beats 2 and 4. That is got an alternate vibe to it! Now attempt the converse: tapping harder on 1 and 3, and delicately on beats 2 and 4.

- Check out Regina Spektor's, *Don't Leave Me.* You can hear the cadence: the calmer bass note occurs on beat 1 and beat 3, and a noisy applaud and catch drum occur on thumps 2 and 4. You'll begin to get a feeling of how music is composed. That is the thing that we call cadence!

- Imagine yourself walking. Every stride will rise to one beat. Those are spoken to musically by quarter notes because in quite a bit of Western music (which means music of the western world, not simply the music of Hank Williams!), there are four of these beats for each measure. Musically, the cadence of your strolling will resemble this:

- Every step is a quarter note. Quarter notes on a music sheet are the strong dark spots that are connected to stems with no banners. You can consider that if you walk: '1, 2, 3, 4-1, 2, 3'

- Quarter notes are alluded to as 'crotchets' in certain spots, for example, the   UK.

- If you were to back your pace off to a large portion of that speed, so you just made a stride every two beats on the 1 and the 3, that would be documented with half notes (for a large portion of a measure). On a sheet of music, half notes appear as though quarter notes, just they aren't strong dark; they are plot in the dark with white centers.

- In a few places, half notes are classified 'minums'.

- If you eased back your pace down considerably, so you just made a stride every four beats, on the one, you would compose that in a general note—or one note for each measure. On a sheet of music, entire notes resemble 'O' or doughnuts, like half notes without stems..

Pick up the pace

Enough of this easing back down. As you noticed, as we eased back the notes, we began removing bits of the note. To begin with, we removed the strong note and we removed the stem. Let's try speed things up. To do that, we are going to add things to the note.

- Go back to our strolling rhythm, and picture that in your psyche (tapping your foot to the beat can help). Presently envision that your transport has recently pulled up to the stop, and you're about a traffic light away. What do you do? You run! What's more, as you run, you attempt to hail the taxi driver.

- To make notes quicker in music, we include a banner. Each banner cuts the time estimation of the note down the middle. For instance, an eighth note (which gets one banner) is 1/2 the estimation of a quarter note; and the sixteenth note (which gets two banners) is 1/2 the estimation of an eighth note. As far as strolling, we go from a walk (quarter note or shake) to a run (eighth note or semiquaver)— twice as quick as a stroll, to a run (sixteenth note or demisemiquaver)— twice as quick as a run.

- Considering that every quarter note is a move as you walk, tap with the example above.

Beam up! As should be obvious with that above model, things can begin to get a touch of befuddling when there are many notes on the page that way. Your eyes begin to cross, and you forget about where you were. To assemble notes into smaller bundles that bode well outwardly, we use radiating.

- Radiating only replaces singular note banners with thick lines drawn between note stems. These are assembled sensibly and keeping in mind that increasingly unpredictable music requires progressively complex radiating standards, for our motivations, we'll shift in gatherings of quarter notes. Contrast the model beneath and the model above. Give tapping a shot to the beat once more and see how much clearer radiating makes the documentation.

- Learn the value of ties and dots. Where a flag will cut the estimation of a note into equal parts, the dot has a comparative work. With constrained special cases the dot is constantly positioned to one side of the note head. At the point when you see a spotted note, that note is expanded by one a large portion of the length of its unique worth.

- For example, a dot put after a half note (least) will be equivalent to the half note in addition to a quarter note. A dot set after a quarter note (crotchet) will be equivalent to a quarter note in addition to an eighth note.

- Ties are like dots—they broaden the estimation of the first note. A tie is just two notes connected along with a bent line between the note heads. In contrast to specks, which are unique and dependent on the estimation of the first note, ties are unequivocal: the note is expanded long by precisely as long as the subsequent note esteem.

- One reason you would use a tie versus a spot is, for instance, when a note's term would not fit musically into the space of a measure (bar). You essentially include the extra span into the following measure as a note and tie the two together.

- Note that the tie is attracted from note head to note head the other way as the stem.

Take a rest.

Some say music is only a progression of notes, and they're half right. Music is a progression of notes and the spaces between them. Those spaces are called rests, and even peacefully, they can truly add movement and life to music. How about we investigate how they're documented.

- Like notes, they have explicit images for explicit lengths. An entire note rest is a square shape sliding from the fourth line, and a half note rest is a square shape lying on the third line and pointing upwards. The quarter note resting is a squiggly line, and the rests are a calculated bar which resembles a number "7" with an indistinguishable number of banners from their identical note value. These banners are constantly clear to one side.

Learning Melody

1. Make sure you understand the above. Now, let's dive into the fun stuff: understanding music! We currently have the basics

down: the staff, the pieces of note, and the fundamentals of notating the duration of notes and rests.

2. Learn the C scale.

The C major scale is the principal scale we use when instructing how to peruse music since the one uses simply normal notes (the white keys on a piano). When you have that secured in your synapses, the rest will follow normally. First, we will show you what it looks like, and then we will show you how to make sense of it and start reading music! Here's what it looks like on the staff. See the 'C scale' above.

- If you investigate the main note, the low C, you'll see that it really goes beneath the staff lines. When that occurs, we just include a staff line for that note—in this way, the little line through the note head. The lower the note, the more staff lines we include. However, we don't have to stress over that now.

- The C scale is comprised of eight notes. These are what might be compared to the white keys on the piano.

- You could have a piano handy, but it's important for you to start to get an idea of what music resembles and what it sounds like.

Learn a little sight-singing—or 'solfège'. That may sound intimidating, but you probably know it already: it's the nicer way of saying 'do, re, mi'.

- By learning to sing the notes you see, you will begin to build a lifelong skill. However, it will be valuable right from the earliest starting point. We should investigate that C scale once more, with the solfege scale included. See the 'C Scale Solfege 11' above.

- You probably already know the Rogers and Hammerstein melody 'Do-Re-Mi' from The Sound of Music. If you can sing the 'do re mi' scale, do that now while you look at the notes.

- Here's a further developed adaptation sing the solfège notes. See the 'C Scale Solfege 1' above.

- Practice singing Solfege—part II a couple of times, until it gets comfortable. Read gradually to enable you to look at each note as you sing it. Then substitute the 'do re mi' for C, D, E. The objective is to sing the genuine notes.

- Remember our note esteems from previously: the high C toward the finish of the mainline, and the low C toward the finish of the subsequent line are half notes, while the remainder of the notes is quarter notes. If you envision yourself strolling, once more, there is a note for each progression. The half notes make two strides.

Reading Music

1. Reading Sharps, Flats, Naturals, and Keys

Take the next step. So far, we've secured the very nuts and bolts of rhythm and melody, and you should have the essential aptitudes vital that you currently understand what every one of those dots and squiggles speaks to. While this may get you through fundamental Flutophone class, there are a couple of more things you'll need to know. Boss among these is key signatures.

In music, you may have seen sharps and flats: sharp looks like a hashtag (sometimes), and a flat resembles a lower-case B (sometimes). They are placed to the left of a note head and show that for a sharp, or a half step lower for a flat, the note to be followed is played a half-step (semitone) higher. As we learned, the C scale comprises the piano's white keys. When you start reading music, it is easier to think of the sharps and flats as the black keys. C major and A minor are without sharps or flats.

2. Know all the tones and all the semitones. Notes are either a whole tone in Western music or a semitone apart. Looking at the C note on the piano keyboard, you can see that there is a black key between it and the next up note, the D. The musical distance between C and D is referred to as a whole ton. The difference between the black-key and the C is called a semitone. Now, you may wonder what this black key is called. The answer to that is, it depends.

If you are going up the scale, a good rule of thumb is the sharp version of the starting note. That note would be the flat version of the starting note when moving down the scale. Therefore, if the black key shifts from C to D, it will be written using a sharp (♯).

- The black note is written in this case as C♯. The black key will be written using a flat (♭) when going down the scale from D to C and use the black note as a passing tone between them.

- These conventions make the lyrics a little easier to interpret. If you were to type up those three notes and use a D♭ instead of a C♯, you would type the notation using a natural sign (♮).

- Notice that there is a new sign—the natural. Whenever you see a natural sign (♮), that implies that the note cancels any sharps or flats previously written. The second and third notes in this model are both 'D's': the first one is a D, and therefore the second D, as it goes up a semitone from the first D, must have the note corrected to show the right note. The more sharps and flats that are scattered around a music sheet, the more musicians have to take in before they can play the score.

Composers who used accidentals in previous measures can also put unnecessary natural signs to give the player clarification. For instance, if a previous measure in a D major piece used an A♯, the next measure using an A can be noted instead with an A-natural.

3. Understand key signatures. So far, we've been taking a look at the C major scale: eight notes, all the white keys, beginning on C. But, you can begin a scale on any note. If you play all the white keys, however, you won't play a significant scale, yet something many refers to as a 'modular scale,' which is past the extent of this article.

- The beginning note, or tonic, is additionally the name of the key. You may have heard someone say, 'It's in the key of C' or something similar. This model implies that the essential scale begins on C and incorporates the notes C D E F G A B C. There is a clear relationship between the notes on a significant scale. Look at the console above.

- Note that between most notes, there is an entire advance. However, there is just a half advance (semitone) among E and F, and among B and C. Each significant scale has this equivalent relationship: the entire half. If you start your scale on G, for instance, it could be composed this way.

- Notice the F♯ close to the top. To keep up the best possible relationship, the F must be raised a semitone with the goal that it's a half advance from the G, not an entire advance. That is sufficiently simple to peruse without anyone else, however, imagine a scenario where you began a significant scale in C♯. (See above.)

- Now it begins to get muddled! To chop down the disarray and make music simpler to peruse, key marks were made. Each significant scale at the very beginning of the music. Looking back at G's main, we see that there's one sharp — F. Instead of placing the sharp on the staff next to the F, we 're pushing it to the left, and from that point on it's just presumed that any F you see will be played as an F.

- This sounds and is played, the same as the G major scale above, with no key signature.

Reading Dynamics and Expression

1. Get loud—or get soft! At the point when you listen to music, you have likely seen that it's not all at a similar volume, constantly. A few sections get extremely loud, and a few sections get extremely delicate. These varieties are known as 'elements'.

   - If the musicality and meter are the core of the music, and notes and keys are the minds, at that point, elements are most likely the voice of the music. Consider the primary form above.

   - Tap out 1 and 2 and 3 and 4 and 5 and 6 and 7 and 8, and so forth (the and is how performers 'state' eighth notes) on your table. Ensure each beat is tapped at a similar pitch, which sounds somewhat like a helicopter. Presently investigate the subsequent variant.

   - Notice the highlight mark (>) over each F note. Tap that out, just this time, highlight each beat that you see the complement mark. Presently, rather than a helicopter, it should sound like a train. With just a shift in accent, we can completely change the character of the music!

2. Play it fortissimo, or piano, or somewhere in between. Just as you're not always speaking at the same level — you're modulating your voice louder or softer depending on the situation — music also modulates in level. How the composer tells the musician what the dynamic markings are intended to be.

- You may see dozens of dynamic markings on a piece of music, but some of the common ones you will find are the letters m,p, and f.

- f means 'forte,' or 'loud'.

- p means 'piano,' or 'softly'.

- m means 'medium' or 'mezzo'. This adjusts the dynamic after it, as in mf, meaning 'medium loud,' or mp, meaning 'medium soft'.

- The softer or louder the music, the more ps or fs you have. Try to sing the above example (using solfège-the first note in this example is the tonic, or 'do'), and use the dynamic markings to spot the difference.

- Get louder, or quieter. Another exceptionally regular unique documentation is the crescendo, and it's the culmination, the decrescendo, or 'diminuendo'. They are visual portrayals of a slow change in volume, which seem as though loosened up '<' and '>' images.

- A crescendo step by step gets stronger, and a decrescendo progressively diminishes the volume. You'll see that, with these two images, the 'open' finish of the image speaks to the stronger dynamic, and the shut end speaks to the quieter dynamic. For instance, if the music directs you to go from forte to piano, you will see an f', then a stretched out '>,' then a 'p'.

- Sometimes, diminuendo or a crescendo will be represented as the shortened words cresc. (crescendo) or dim. (diminuendo).

Advancing

1. Keep learning!

Learning how to read music resembles learning the alphabet. The nuts and bolts take a short time to learn and are genuinely simple. However, there are such a significant number of subtleties, ideas, and aptitudes that you can discover to keep you learning for a lifetime. A few arrangers even venture to such an extreme as to compose music on staff lines that structure spirals or designs, or even use no staff! This article should give you a decent basis to continue developing!

2. Learn these key signatures. There is a minimum of one for every note on the scale—and the savvy student will see that there are 2 keys for the same note in some cases. For example, the key of G♯ sounds the same as the key of A♭! When playing the piano— and for this article, the difference is academic. However, some composers—especially those that write for strings—suggest that the A♭ is played a little flatter than the G♯. Here are the main signatures for the major scales:

- Keys using sharps: A, E, G, D, B, F♯, C♯

- Keys not using sharps or flats: C

- Keys using flats: F, A♭, D♭, B♭, E♭, G♭, C♭

- As you can see above, when you move through the sharp key signatures, you add sharpness one by one until each note is played sharply in the C key. You will add flats as you move through the flat key signatures until each note is played flat in the C key.

- Knowing that composers typically write in key signatures that are easy for the player to read may be of some comfort. D major is a very common key to playing string instruments as the open strings are related to the tonic, D. There are few works that have strings playing in E, either minor or brass playing E major-writing is as much a pain as reading it is for you.

THE STAFF

The journey of figuring out how to read sheet music begins with the staff. The staff is the arrangement of five-level lines on which notes are set in standard violin sheet music.

There are seven notes of which all music is based: A, B, C, D, E, F, and G. When you get to G, you will begin back once again with A and the cycle would repeat, getting higher in pitch as you go up the staff.

There are additionally different pitches that relate with a similar letter in music. For example, there are a few diverse A's on the violin. They are simply in differing types of high or low pitches.

The Notes on the Lines

The easiest way to learn notes from violin music is to divide the personnel into lines and spaces.

These are the notes that fall on staff lines, meaning the notes directly on top of the lines, intersecting them with the lines.

Beginning from the baseline, start to remember each note going up the top line. One famous memory aide you may have heard is 'Each Good Boy Does Fine'. Another is 'Elvis' Guitar Broke Down Friday'.

These gadgets can be extremely convenient to assist you with remembering the notes! You can also begin with an amateur violin book, for example, *Essential Elements for Strings Volume I.* It will give you some incredible activities to assist you with remembering and becoming familiar with these notes.

The Notes on the Spaces

Next, there are the notes of violin music falling between the lines-on the spaces:

Another incredible mental aide applies here. If you take a look at the notes beginning from the base note up to the top note, you'll see that the letters spell F-A-C-E. What's more, that rhymes with space. It's very infectious and vital: 'Face is in the space!'

When you're practicing or working from an activity book, make a point to remember these mnemonic devices in mind. If you overlook the name of a note, first decide if the note falls on a line or space.

Then, take your finger or a pencil and point to each note from the base on up while speaking them out loud, using your mental helper as an aide. It couldn't be any more obvious, figuring out how to read violin notes isn't that difficult!

Ledger Lines

The five lines and four spaces aren't exactly enough to contain the whole range of violin notes. To put these violin music notes, we use little lines or runs called 'record lines'. The notes can fall in the spaces or on the lines between them, simply like the five lines of the staff.

In the G scope diagram above, you'll notice that different notes fall underneath the staff (lower in pitch) or more (higher in pitch.)

To read these notes, you can use the ones on the staff that you know as a source of perspective to make sense of them.

Significant Symbols on the Staff

A significant piece of figuring out how to read violin notes is retaining the various images you may run over on the staff. You'll notice some new symbol at the start of each staff line if you investigate some violin sheet music or an activity book.

THE TREBLE CLEF

You may perceive the extravagant swirly symbol toward the start of the staff as a clef. Clef symbol as a reference focuses on the name a particular note on the staff from which the names of the various notes are based.

Lower pitched instruments use different clefs with various reference focuses, for example, bass or alto clef. In violin (just as more pitched instruments, for example, flute and trumpet), we use the treble clef.

The primary concern a learner should take from this is in case you're taking a look at sheet music with a treble clef on it. It shows that the music is reasonable to be played on the violin.

Key Signature

Next, you'll see the key mark, which is imperative to focus on as it will tell you whether you have any flat or sharp notes in the melody.

- A flat note (for example B flat) is a half-advance low in pitch than the base note (B) and is implied by this image: ♭

- A sharp note (for example C sharp) is a half-advance higher in pitch than the base note (C) and is implied by this image: #

- If you see a flat symbol in the key mark, take a look at the line or space that is striking through the focal point of the image and figure out which note relates to the line or space.

Presently all through the term of the piece (regardless of whether it's high or low of that note), you will play the flat form of that note. The equivalent goes for when you see a sharp image in the key mark. Investigate the sharp image and notice that there is a little slanted square in the center of the symbol.

Whichever note compares to the line or space that the square structures around will be the note that will turn out to be sharp all through the piece.

Some of the time, there will be different sharps or a mix of sharps and pads. If you don't notice any sharps or pads in your key mark, you can simply expect that all the notes in the piece will be your ordinary or 'natural' notes.

Any notes that are not referenced in the key signature are thought to be normal notes too.

Time Signature

Next is the timing signature. The timing signature tells you how to check a piece or what number of beats are in each measure.

Vertical lines partition the staff into fragments called 'measures,' which contain a specific number of beats based on what your timing scheme says.

The top number in the timing scheme tells you what number of beats are in each measure. When the distributed number of beats have been checked out, it's an ideal opportunity to proceed onward to the following measure and begin the tallying once more.

The base number depicts the length of the beat. If you have a four on the base (generally normal), that would mean that you are basing your beat off of the length of a quarter note.

These are the numbers you'll be seeing on the bottom of the time signature and which note lengths they correspond to:

- 2 = half note

- 4 = quarter note

- 8 = eighth note

- 16 = sixteenth note

These are the most common time signatures you will see:

The 4/4 timing signature is basic to the point that it is alluded to as 'common time' and frequently, you will see a C on the music where the timing scheme would typically be which intends to play the piece in 4/4 time.

TYPES OF MUSICAL NOTES

One of the main places to begin when studying music is to find out all the sorts of melodic notes. Knowing the names of every one of these notes, just as their time esteems, how to draw them, and what the pieces of the notes are called is vital to have the option to read music well.

Music Note Names And Their Time Values

A musician needs to know how long each sound can play for when playing music.

Composers tell them by using different note symbols. Let us look at some of the types of music notes that you certainly need to know while learning how to read music.

Semibreve (whole note) 4 Beats

The first note is a semibreve or a 'whole note' as it's called in the US. It's like a letter O or small oval-shaped zero, which is a good way of thinking about it when you start writing music first.

We call that oval-shaped part of note the head of note.

A semibreve has a 4-beat value.

That means we count to four while holding the note when we play a semibreve.

Minim (half note) 2 Beats

The second note we 're going to look at is a minimal or 'half note.'

It is similar to a semibreve but has a line coming from its note head's right-hand side.

That line is known as a stem.

The stem halves the note 's value, so a minim has a two-beat value.

That means that we count to two, half as long as a semibreve when we play a minim.

Crotchet (quarter note) 1 Beats

Next, we have a 'quarter note' or crotchet.

It's like a minim, but it's filled in black with its note head.

This again halves the note value, and so a crotchet has one beat value, half as long as a minimum.

Quaver (eighth note) ½ Beats

This note is an eighth note, or quaver.

It's like a crotchet, but there's also a tail coming from its stem 's side.

The tail of the note is often called a flag or a pin.

The tail again halves the note 's value, and so a quaver has a half-beat value, half as long as a crotchet.

Semiquaver (16th note) ¼ Beats

We've got a semiquaver or 'sixteenth note' next up.

It's like a quaver, but it's got two tails coming from its stem.

That means its half the quaver value and so it's worth one-quarter of a beat.

Demisemiquaver (32nd note) 1/8 Beats

A demisemiquaver, also known as a '32nd note' is available here. It has three tails (one more than one semiquaver).

A demisemiquaver is worth half a semiquaver 's value and thus is worth one-eighth of a crotchet beat.

Other Notes

These are the main notes that you will find and use in musical notation, but you can also get longer and shorter notes.

Hemidemisemiquaver (64th note)

A hemidemiquaver (I know it's a bit mouthful) or in the US it's called a '64th note' is just like a demisemiquaver but with an extra tail.

It is very rare though so don't think too much about it!

You can get shorter notes than this, like the semihemidemisemiquaver (128th note) and the demisemihemidemisemiquaver (256th note), but I'm not going to cover those because they're extremely rare.

Breve (double whole note)

Also, you can have a note called a'double whole note' or breve worth eight beats, twice as long as a semibreve.

It's also quite uncommon, but for a grade 5 music theory exam, you'll need to know about it.

The Musical Note

Sometimes the note values are represented as a tree or as a pyramid. This is known as the tree of music note and is a great way to visualize the relationship between all the values of note.

The Tree of Notes for Music (UK terminology)

Note Stems

As well as being able to point the stems of notes upwards they may also point downwards. When the stem of a note points upwards, it comes from the right side of the head of the note.

But, if the stem of a note points downwards, it comes from the note head's left side.

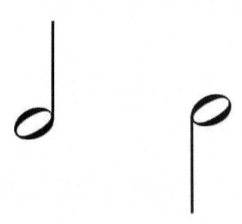

However, there are some guidelines to learn about which direction the stems should be pointing. I'll cover some of the basics about stave notes in this article here.

However, the most important thing is to have the stem always on the appropriate side of the head of the note.

Note Tails

Note tails function very differently from notes that have tails such as quavers and semiquavers.

The tails of the note always come from the stem's right-hand side, regardless of whether or not they point up or down.

The way to note that is that the tails still follow the music's course. To put it another way, we are reading music from left to right. So the tails of the note always point toward the music ...

To the left.

Beaming notes together

When we have at least two notes with a tail (like quavers and semiquavers) close to one another, we combine their tails with a beam between the highest points of their stems.

This is to help make it simpler for performers to read the notes.

How about we see how to pillar trembles.

beaming quavers (eighth notes)

At when we beam quavers together, we combine the stems using their note tails.

For instance, two trembles all alone become:

There are many rules and conventions concerning how many quavers we can beat together. But on grouping notes in different time signatures, I will cover those in another post.

Semiquavers to beam (sixteenth notes)

It functions the same with semiquavers, but instead, we use two beams instead of using one beam between their stems.

This is because there are two tails in them.

Depending on how many tails the note has, we will only add beam or two for demisemiquavers and hemidemiquavers.

Combinations, semiquavers and of quavers

We can also beam together different combinations of quavers and semiquavers. For instance:

There are some rules on how to beam and group notes in various time signatures.

Dotted notes

Sometimes a composer might wish to make a note last longer than the value of a note when writing music. If this is the case, we can use a dotted note to extend the note duration.

This dot makes the note longer by half its value after the head of note. A dotted minim, for example, has the same time value as a minimum plus a crotchet:

$$\text{𝅗𝅥.} \quad = \quad \text{𝅗𝅥} \quad + \quad \text{♩}$$

Or a dotted quaver is equivalent to a semiquaver plus a quaver.

$$\text{♪.} \quad = \quad \text{♪} \quad + \quad \text{♪}$$

However, we cannot have a dotted mark going over a line of rows. If we want a note to go over a line of bars, then we'll use a tied note which we'll look at next.

Tied notes

A tie is a sloped line uniting two notes which are next to each other and have the same pitch. This line looks like the one below.

When you see a tie, it means adding the time values of the notes to create a longer note. Two minims tied together, for example, have the same value as a semibreve:

Two crotchets tied together have the same value as a minim:

They don't have to be the same time value either. You could have a crotchet tied to a quaver or a minim tied to a crotchet etc.

NAMES OF THE STRINGS ON THE VIOLIN

Commit The Violin Strings To Memory

Learning the four strings on the violin is a significant advance in our learning procedure. It's straightforward, it's fun, and it's important to our capacity to tune, our capacity to play, and our capacity to improve our abilities on the violin.

Below Are The Names Of The Violin's Strings

G

This is the thickest string on the violin and is therefore the most reduced in pitch. It is situated on the left half of the violin (for right handed players, on the correct side of the violin for left handed players). The D string is directly close to the G string.

D

This is one of the inside two strings on the violin.

It is the second thickest string. It is situated next to the G string on the right-hand side of the violin (for left handed players, on the left hand side of the violin for right handed players), which is the simplest way to remember it.

A string is on the other side of the D string.

A

The A is found directly close to the E string, on the left side of the violin (for left-handed players, on the right half of the violin for right handed players.) This is the most straightforward approach to recollect its location.

E

The E string is the thinnest and along these lines highest pitched string on the violin. It is situated on the correct side of the violin (for right handed players, on the left half of the violin for left handed players.)

Another approach to find the E string is that when you hold the violin up to your shoulder, the E string is uppermost path from your head.

NOTES OF THE VIOLIN AND FINGER POSITIONS

A look at violin finger placement and notes. Two fundamental concepts that you must understand if you want to be good at playing the violin.

Violin notes and finger positioning are two simple principles that you need to grasp if you want to be able to play the violin to a good standard. You need to learn how to read violin notes and the position of each violin string notes as well.

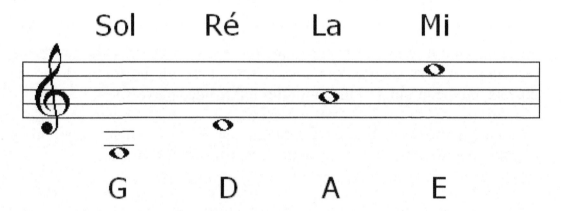

Where are the Notes on a Violin?

Start by having references to violin note diagrams (such as the ones in this article) and memorize each note 's position. We'll go over how to use tapes in this post to help you make things simpler, but for now, having the right basic understanding of location is what you should be concentrating on.

Begin by practicing the first position until you get that down.

The first position uses the most minimal five notes on each string. This is trickier than it sounds because getting the position even a little offbase means that the note won't sound right. So to make things simpler for you when you are learning, you can put tapes on the violin.

When you have sufficiently trained, your fingers will instinctually know where to put themselves, and the tapes can be removed. How about we take a look at intonation.

What is Intonation?

Intonation is the where you place your fingers on the strings. This finger position affects the pitch of the notes that you play – that is, regardless of whether they have a higher pitch, or a lower one. Pitch is critical because it influences how great the piece will end up sounding.

You will manage half-steps and full steps. If a note is set apart with a #, it means that it is sharp, that is, one half-step greater than the normal note would be.

When a note is set apart with a ♭, it means that it is level, i.e. one half-advance lower than the ordinary note would be.

As you are learning to play the violin, you should have gotten yourself some violin fingering charts. Remember these before you begin to play with the goal that you remember all the violin finger positions. That way, you will know where to put your fingers and get the intonation directly from the very first moment.

Using Finger Tapes

Begin by guaranteeing that your violin has been appropriately tuned. There are cell phone applications or particular gadgets that you can use to help with this. Check before putting the tapes on or you may wind up with inappropriate notes without knowing it.

Beginning at the top fingerboard on the G string, move about two inches along the string to a spot and then pluck it out. Test the tuner to ensure the note on the tuner reads as A.

Now take a pencil and imprint the spot. At that point put a three-inch tape strip in position along the spot but under the strings. Ensure that it holds solidly to the violin.

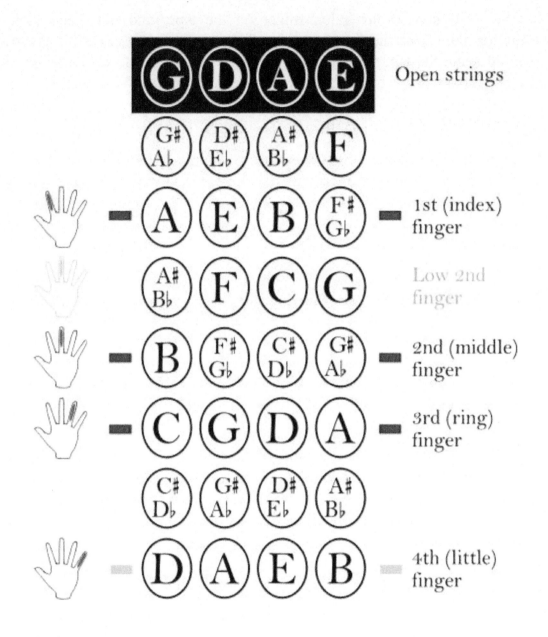

Open strings

1st (index) finger

Low 2nd finger

2nd (middle) finger

3rd (ring) finger

4th (little) finger

Check the Index Finger

Now hold down your index finger on the tape, and pull each string individually. Check the tuner to ensure the tuner is showing an A. If so, you should leave the tape where it is, otherwise you might need to change its location. For every tape you put this process will be followed.

The Second Finger

Begin this one about an inch from where you place the first piece of tape. Follow the same process as above. This time, the G string should show up as B on your tuner.

Your Ring Finger

This is up to a limit of an a large portion of an inch from where you place the second piece of tape. The G string should appear as C on your tuner.

The Pinky

This one is about an inch from where you place the third piece of tape, and you should move it along the string until D is shown by your tuner.

Violin Notes and Finger Placement

Now, you have an understanding of violin notes and finger placement; you have somewhere to begin. It is enticing to attempt to rehearse various positions at the same time, yet you will advance significantly better if you adhere to the main position while you are learning.

This allows you to decide on your strategy without stressing over changing finger positions excessively.

From that point on, you should simply rehearse each day until your fingers fly over the fingerboard without you thinking about it.

HOW TO TUNE THE VIOLIN

The violin has four strings that are tuned in fifths. This is down to a high scientific pitch of the strings is G3, D4, A4, and E5.

The violin is tuned in perfect fifths-each string is tuned a perfect fifth interval from the string (or cords) next to it. The violin strings are tightened or loosened, so the pegs and fine tuners produce the right note. Some violins have only fine tuners on the E string while others have fine tuners on all four strings. If you purchase a violin with just one fine tuner, you have the option of having a luthier install the other three fine tuners in the tailpiece. As their names imply, if the string is off pitch by a small interval of no more than half a tone or so, the fine tuners are used to tune the string. When the string is out of tune by half a tone, then the pegs are initially used to tune the note. Afterward, the fine tuner is used to ensure that the note is actually in order. Beginners are typically prompted not to tune with the pegs except, if it is essential, to maintain a strategic distance from pointless string breakages. If you are starting to tune from the peg, it is a good idea to tune with a logical tuner to ensure you are not over-fixing the string, anyway with most low-end logical tuners must be careful about tuning an octave excessively high or excessively low. Just move the peg around a couple of millimeters one after another - you will be astonished at how a little turn can influence the string's pitch!

- Tuning the Violin

- Tuning using a Piano

- Relative Tuning

- Tuning with Electronic Violin Tuners

- Alternate Tunings for the Violin

- Common tuning Problems

- Quick-Reference Tuning Tips

Tuning the Violin

When tuning any instrument, you should consistently tune from beneath the note up. This prevents string breakages and organizes the way toward tuning, so you become progressively acquainted with the sound of an ideal, in-order string. When tuning your violin, you should also consistently tune using the fine tuners whenever the situation allows (most student violins should have fine tuners). At the point when a fine tuner has been twisted directly down to the end of the screw, slacken the fine tuner right to the end of the screw before cautiously fixing the tuning peg. This way, you keep the string from being over-fixed.

When you are tuning your violin, play the note constantly with your bow and listen cautiously to the string as it fixes towards the ideal pitch. Keep in mind that you may need to stop to tune partially through training, particularly if you are using new strings as they will stretch and may require fixing from the peg on numerous occasions per practice.

It is prudent to begin by tuning the A string first, trailed by the D, G, then E strings. At the point when you begin to turn out to be increasingly acquainted with the sound of the notes of the various strings, you can have a go at tuning the strings against one another - this is known as relative tuning (see 'Relative Tuning' area).

If you need to find out about the material science of tuning any instrument, head over to The Science of Tuning Musical Instruments.

Tuning using a Piano

Tuning your violin using a piano or keyboard is a moderately straightforward undertaking. The image above shows the piano keys that compare with the strings on the violin. Ensure you use the 'Center C' on the image as a source of perspective, so you don't attempt to tune your violin an octave excessively low or excessively high. Play the note on the piano and match the right string to the note. Make sure to use the fine tuners on your violin to tune if the string is out by a portion of a tone. Use the pedals on the piano so the note you play can sound uninhibited, so you can have two hands accessible to tune the violin.

Relative Tuning

Relative tuning is a technique for tuning the violin to itself and is an ability that requires a lot of time and training. First and foremost, a few people think that it's simpler to hear the genuine pitch of the note by shutting their eyes and inclining their left ear towards the F openings. You can attempt this as well while you tune your violin. If you have seen an ensemble play live, you may have seen the symphony go around the A. The A string is played by the concertmaster (lead violinist) to ensure all individuals and segments of the symphony are tuned appropriately. As a violinist, you use the A that is 'went' to you to tune your different strings. To do this, you first ensure the A string is in order to play the A and D strings together, tuning in for the ideal fifth stretch to ring in order. At that point, play the D and G strings together, followed at last by the A and E. To tune like this, you should have decent information or what the strings sound like, and what an ideal fifth seems like as well. Flawless fifths will sound resounding, so you might have the option to tune, thusly if you listen cautiously to the ringing sound, or by taking a look at how the strings vibrate when you play them together. Begin tuning in for these notes when you tune as an amateur as it is an incredible aptitude to have the option to disguise a set note and understand the specific ideal recurrence of the note by ear.

Tuning with Electronic Violin Tuners

Alternate Tunings for the Violin

Generally, alternate tunings for the violin are used by violinists. However, country and fiddle violinists employ a range of alternate tunings to suit the music style they play. Some country musicians prefer tuning their violin in fourths instead of fifths, while others may cross-tune the violin to suit the music style they play. The violin features a variety of different cross-tunings. For the violin, the most common cross-tuning is when the D string to E and the G string is tuned to an A so that the A-E-A-E tunes the violin strings from lowest to highest. The tuning of the A-E-A-E is most frequently used for songs in A major. Playing in D major may also cross-tune the violin to the A-D-A-E tuning (again from the lowest to the highest), where the G-string is raised one tone higher. There are several other less popular alternate tunings for the violin, most of which will only be used in American folk/fiddle music.

As a beginner, you should begin to learn the violin with standard tuning as standardized tuning gives the instrument a better sound and is easier to learn.

Common tuning Problems

The most well-known issue when tuning pegs that sneak out of the spot. To fix this difficulty, have a go at loosening up the peg a round or two and afterward fix the peg once more, squeezing the peg sensibly hard into the pegbox while turning the peg. Ideally, the peg will stick, and your violin will remain in order!

If you wound the fine tuners down to the stub and can't screw anymore, you can fix it by first winding the fine tuner back to the extent that it drops out. Then, fix the string at the peg, close to a couple of millimeters one after another, until the pitch is simply under the correct note you need. At that point, you can keep on tuning the string at the fine tuner. This technique for resetting the fine tuners will keep the string from breaking or wearing out because of overabundance fixing. If you discover that you over-turn the peg and the string, at that point sounds higher than it should, you can loosen up the peg somewhat to fix this as you won't have the option to used the loosened up fine tuner to tune down.

If you have difficulty with slipping pegs or if you find that your fine tuners are difficult to turn, examine our Violin Maintenance Guide to find out about what you can do to fix these issues.

Quick-Reference Tuning Tips

Tuning a violin is quite easy if you follow these few tips:

- Top Tip: Remember to consistently tune from beneath the note to keep strings from breaking.

- Use the fine tuners, to prevent string breakages. At the point when they become slowed down to the stub, relax them right the route up, use the peg to fix the string to simply underneath the note, and use the fine tuners to adjust the note the remainder of the way. Don't over fix the string at the peg as you won't have the option to tune down with the free fine tuners.

- Tune the A string first, trailed by D, G, then E strings. This is how symphonic violinists tune their violins. It helps to get into a decent tuning of everyday practice.

If you are using a tuner at that point, have a go at murmuring the right note from the tuner first before you tune to know precisely what note you are searching for. If you can't arrive at the note with your voice, simply envision murmuring it, this has a lot of a similar impact.

HOW TO HOLD THE VIOLIN

The Shoulder Rest

My technique revolves around having a shoulder rest that is secure in its situation on the rear of the violin. The objective of the shoulder rest is to prop up the violin and to make it with the goal that the violin is secure on the shoulder. We don't need is an excessively high shoulder rest. This is a general issue for my younger students. The shoulder rest should mean that you don't need to bring down your jaw too far to sit on the chin rest.

However, if the rest of your shoulder is so high that you need to uncomfortably raise your head above usual comfortable levels, you either need to change the rest of your shoulder or find a better suitable shoulder rest.

The aim is always the same if you use a violin sponge and rubber bands, inflatable shoulder rest, or a plastic shoulder rest with feet.

There are various types of should-rests, some better than others. Ignore the shoulder rest targets, and if yours don't help the violin and secure it on the neck, it's time to look for a new shoulder rest.

If you find yourself needing a shoulder rest, check out our article on the subject. We hope it helps you!

THE VIOLIN MANTRA: 'NOSE SCROLL TOES'

I have my student recollect a mantra of sorts. Repeat after me, 'Nose, Scroll, Toes.' 'Nose, Scroll, Toes.' First, we should simply manage 'Nose, Scroll.'

Keep in mind; we need the CHIN to sit on the chin rest. This means our nose will be, pointing toward our parchment. This is the right method to hold the violin.

You will see a few violinists who play various styles of music who don't cling to this strategy for playing. Notwithstanding, 'Nose, Scroll, Toes' is the RULE. When you know the principles, and you are generally excellent at them, you can approach breaking them.

I suggest that while you are learning the instrument, you figure out how to play following this truism as this will be the ideal route for you to play your instrument. It will even assist you with reading sheet music later!

HOW HARD SHOULD MY CHIN PRESS ON THE SHOULDER REST OF THE VIOLIN?

You shouldn't have to press your chin rest very hard to keep the violin in place, as long as you're having a rest on your shoulder. Generally speaking, if your chin hurts, or your muscles become locked up from pressing down on the chin rest, you are pushing your chin rest too hard.

My rule is as follows: play with how much pressure you place on the chin rest (and your shoulder rest on the bottom side of the violin), by putting your hand under the violin in case you drop it.

Next, slowly release pressure from your chin on the chin rest. Just before the violin begins to dip from a lack of pressure on the chin rest is how hard you should be pressing down.

KEEP YOURSELF LEVEL-HEADED

Your head and your violin should be level. This means when holding your violin, the scroll should not be pointing at the floor or pointing at the roof. The scroll ought to be totally corresponding to the floor and the roof. Along these lines, you will ensure your stance is most appropriate for future strategies.

WHERE DO I PUT MY HAND ON THE VIOLIN?

Start by simply holding the violin on the upper side of the violin across from your chin. This should be the closest upper bout to your string E. It is just as simple as this. This is how I learn to play open strings for my students.

The next way to carry the violin is by placing the hand next to the nut, just in front of the peg. There are two main things to get your hand on the violin.

1) Your left hand's first finger base knuckle, where the base of the finger becomes the bulk of the hand, should be on the side of the fingerboard next to the E string. 2) Your left-hand thumb should be on the opposite side of the violin near the G string.

Find a point halfway between the tip of your thumb and the first knuckle after the tip. That halfway/middle point is where you should make contact with the side of the fingerboard of the violin neck.

Next, you want the crevice between the thumb and the first finger to be open. Don't let the violin neck slide down and touch the fleshy part of your hand.

WHAT SHOULD I DO WITH MY WRIST?

Following this, make sure that your wrist is rotated so that your pinky finger is facing you. Also, the wrist needs to be straight. Don't let it become bent and flat.

You'll know it's incorrect because it will resemble the hand you use to push something or hold up a tray. I tell my students, 'no pizza waiter hand!'. Don't get me wrong; I LOVE pizza and their waiters. But we're playing the violin, not working at a pizzeria.

YOUR ELBOW SHOULD REST DIRECTLY UNDER THE VIOLIN

Finally, ensure the left elbow is legitimately underneath the violin. By no means will the elbow be behind the violin.

Your elbow should be underneath the strings of the instrument. On occasion playing the G and D strings, you will really push your elbow forward towards the E string.

I realize it sounds odd; however, trust me, it causes you with additional finger length that this way will assist you with playing notes more easily.

Fingering And Positions

There are several violin finger positions one must learn. However, as a beginner, the first you'll need to learn is called the first position. This is the violin fingering chart we have shown previously.

The first position incorporates the first (or most minimal) five notes that you can play on every violin string. Since violins don't have frets or marks that give you where to put your fingers the manner in which guitars do, one of the most testing parts of learning the instrument is knowing where to put your fingers. The violin fingering diagram can help with this.

However, if you don't have your finger in precisely the correct spot (regardless of whether it's slightly off), the note can come out sounding of tune. To help with this, a few instructors favor putting finger tapes on the fingerboard that show you the best possible violin finger position.

After some time, your fingers will create something we call 'muscle memory,' and inevitably, you'll have the option to remove the tapes and play in order without them. Remembering the notes on the violin's fingering outline will help you learn all your first position notes.

Double Ropes

Since the violin has four strings, you can immediately play on two strings by putting the bow on both strings while using the appropriate fingering. This is shown in sheet music as two notes stacked on one another.

Pizzicato

This is the Italian word for pinch and can also be translated to mean plucked. Violins and other stringed instruments, such as the cello or viola, are traditionally played with a bowing method (arco). Pizzicato intends to pluck the strings rather, and this is ordinarily finished with your index finger.

Vibrato

Vibrato violin is a strategy often used by experienced violinists to draw attention to their music by oscillating the note around the base pitch. Most violinists only begin to learn vibrato after having had a relatively solid tone without vibrato and reaching a certain level of ease with the left hand.

Harmonics

A harmonic played on an open string. A finger contacts the string gently at one of its nodes. Nodes are placed on the string, where its partial vibrations develop. Accordingly, the whole string, and not simply the fingered part, vibrates along a few equivalent lengths—an incomplete sound rather than the basic. Common sounds up to the fifth halfway are called for. Higher music is required only in exceptional conditions.

Bow technique

Hold the bow properly. How you hold the bow determines the angle and pressure of the bow on the strings. ...

Keep your elbow at a right-angle. ...

Keep that bow in the middle - and the middle. ...

Keep the bow flat on the strings.

USEFUL TIPS

- Pay attention to your posture and adjust your music stand to the right height. Correct posture allows you to play the violin better and avoid physical problems and ailments.

- Always devote yourself to tuning before playing the violin. In this regard, there are free apps that will facilitate your work, such as the *Cleartune* application, or alternatively, you could get a tuner.

- Find the areas where you feel the most tension and find out the cause. If you have pain in your jaw maybe you are pressing your chin too hard on the instrument, if you have pain in the arm with which you hold the bow, it is possible that you are raising your shoulder too much.

- To play the violin you must hold the bow in the right way; the index finger must be placed on the handle between the silver band and the heel.

- Always keep your hand relaxed and concave as if it contains an object. In the beginning it will be difficult to play the violin whilst thinking about all of this, therefore you will have to pay constant attention to it throughout your practicing.

- Avoid growing your nails too much, they hinder the execution and could damage the strings.

- The first few times you may feel a slight pain in your hands when you finish playing the violin, but it's all about habit. You can massage them and gradually increase the practice time, so as not to tire yourself too much.

- If you have decided to play the violin while sitting, don't choose a chair that's too soft, otherwise you may lose the correct posture and will tend to curve your back.

- To play the violin it is necessary to place the instrument on the clavicle and not on the shoulder.

- Although some recommend the use of the chin rest, while others strongly advise against it, this tool could be very useful to those who are just starting to play the violin, because it relieves shoulder pain. In the future, you can choose whether to continue using it.

- To learn to use the bow you need to hold it gently without squeezing, with the little finger positioned on the smoothest part and the fingers set at the same distance apart.

- If you are still a beginner, be careful not to 'crush' the strings with the bow. When you start playing the violin you will often make the mistake of pressing on the strings when you should be plucking them with the bow instead. If you want to intensify the power of the sound, just use the weight of your arm that holds the bow in your hand.

SHEET MUSIC

On the following pages you will find the sheet music of the following popular songs:

- Twinkle, Twinkle, Little Star

- Canon in D

- Jingle Bells

- Minuet

- Hush Little Baby

- London Bridge

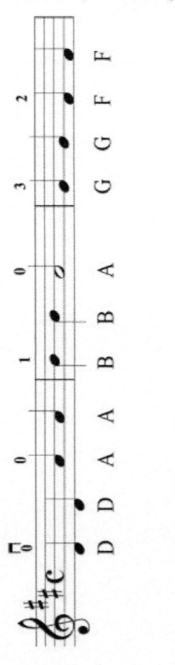

82

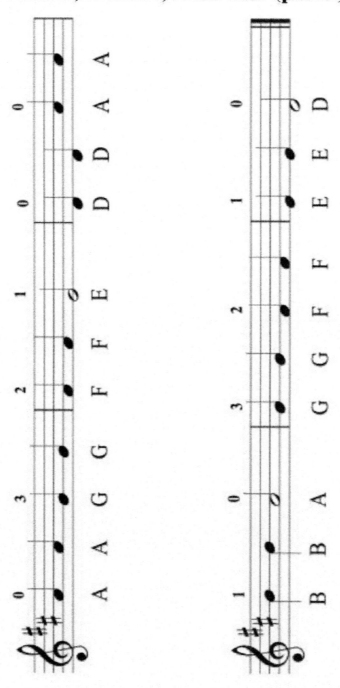

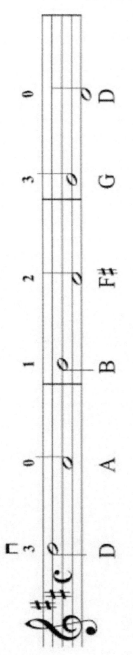
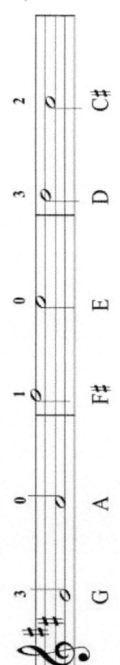

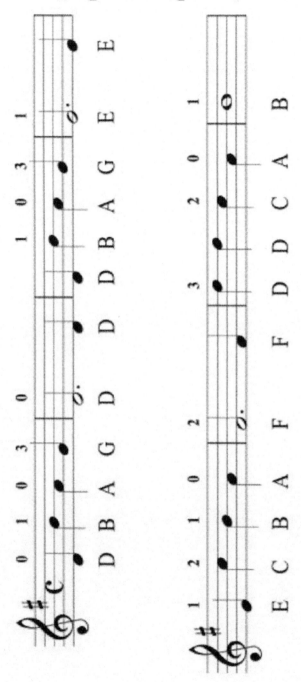

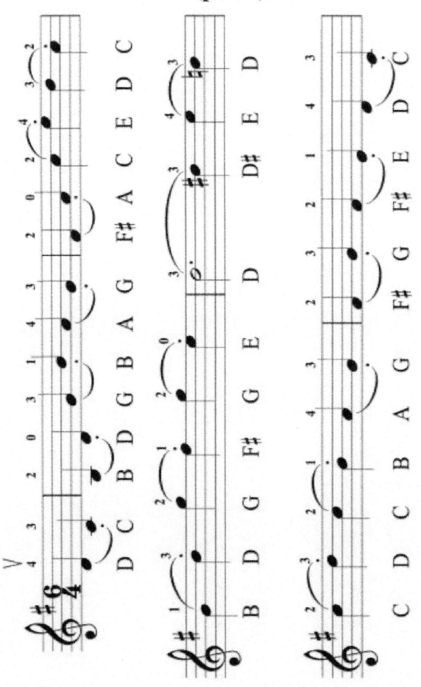

96

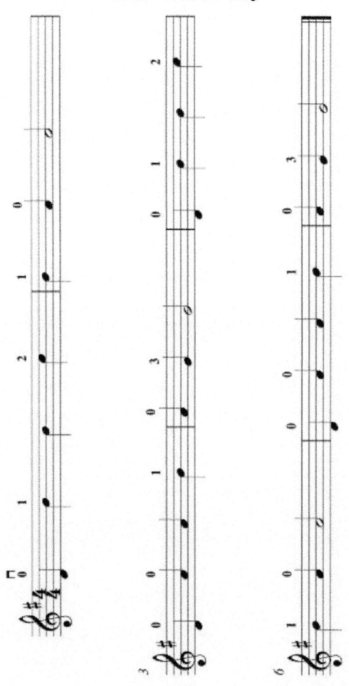

98

100

CONCLUSION

In conclusion, considering the historical backdrop of the violin permits unique

viewpoints to acoustical researches.

Specific arching has created within the first decade of the sixteenth century with bended bridges to play strings independently, simultaneously as the new family of various sizes of violins was built up to play various pieces of orchestral music.

Solid body went with a firm arched bow and scaffolds that were woody. The playing was that of ensemble music.

The wooden string was an invention around 1660-1680 that permitted the innovation of the violoncello and facilitated the change of bowing thin and thick strings.

Composers exploited these new characteristics and wrote for solo violin and cello.

The impact of flatter arching in relation comparable to adaptability of the body was a component created around 1700. It is related with an alternate violin playing presented by sonatas and concertos for solo violins. It presented longer bow from impacts of long and short, increasingly slow bow strokes, bouncing and right hand methods. This expanded demands for thinner violin and cello necks for the speed of fingering and shift in higher positions, and the advanced neck shows up in a several phases between 1760.

Bows develop between 1740 and 1790 and raised to the present-day bow that is going to enhance the expressive chance of romantic music.

Nineteenth century's bridges got more slender and increasingly open, presumably progressively adaptable. If the distinctive state of every one of these settings where to be tried independently connected to their particular turn of events, we could have an alternate comprehension of why the producers, after numerous investigations, embraced this or another shape for an angling, a bow, a fingerboard, a bridge.

Working by experimentation for the performers, they followed their necessities and requests to fulfill the music of their time, to open prospects to writers and instrumentalists. The acoustical properties of these things can't be completely understood if they are not identified with the section of varieties they were permitted, so as to be set and coupled to a particular instrument for a particular music. Likewise, they were adjusted for curving space between ff holes, bass bars also, strings that are not anymore in used today.

Printed in Great Britain
by Amazon

36923523R00066